Unless otherwise indicated, all Scripture quotations are taken from The Holy Bible KJV, Cambridge Edition: 1769; King James Version Bible Online, 2015. http://www.kingjamesbible.org. Used by permission. All rights reserved.

Scripture quotations are taken from the Holy Bible, New International Version®, NIV®. Copyright © 1973, 1978, 1984, 2011 by Biblica, Inc. ™ Used by permission of Zondervan. All rights reserved worldwide. www.zondervan.com The "NIV" and "New International Version" are trademarks registered in the United States Patent and Trademark Office by Biblica, Inc.

Scripture quotations are from the ESV® Bible (The Holy Bible, English Standard Version®), copyright © 2001 by Crossway, a publishing ministry of Good News Publishers. Used by permission. All rights reserved.

Copyright © 2021 by George A. Gee

Barracks Editorial & Design House, LLC:
iambevtheeditor@gmail.com

What Happened to the Preacher

Printed in the United States of America. All rights reserved. Contents or any portion thereof may not be reproduced in whole or in part without the author's express written consent except for the use of brief quotations in a book review. Please direct all inquiries to Georgegee572@yahoo.com .

ISBN-978-0-578-92890-6

Printed in the United States of America

DEDICATION

I dedicate this disquisition to prognosticators, who participate in the foolishness of preaching. In the hope, it will strengthen and encourage, giving wisdom and insight into the paths of eternal life.

Eternity is immensely a long time; therefore, make ready.

CONTENTS

DEDICATION...iii

FOREWORD vii

INTRODUCTION ix

ONE "Behold the Lamb of God".........................11

TWO *"God's Business"* 25

THREE *"Fresh Oil"* 35

FOUR *"Old School"* 47

FIVE "Suicide" 55

SIX "What's with the Black Preacher?" 67

SEVEN "When Humility Kissed Holiness" 77

EIGHT "Satan's Seat"............................85

NINE "When Preachers Pray" 95

TEN "Hugs Heal" 109

About the Author 121

FOREWORD

George Andrew Gee, affectionately known as the "Apostle of Love," has always been a loving person as far back as when we attended Bible College together, pursuing our degrees in Theology as young aspiring preachers.

Apostle Gee has now debuted in the literary arena with "What Happened to The Preacher." I like this book because the author shares with us the ultrasound of his life testimony. He shows us the heartbeat of his vision as an inspiring young preacher and the latter trimesters of hardships as a man of God and then finally birth the challenge to future preachers by encouraging them to stay true to the written Word of God in a humanistic culture.

I was encouraged by this book to continue fighting the good fight of faith while at the same time staying true to the authenticity of the written inspired Word of God. I recommend this book to any preacher with the call of God on their lives and that they share a copy with a friend as a gift for constant reference when life gets "complicated," and if you live long enough at some point, it will. What Happened to The Preacher is a must-read.

Rev. Dr. Alandus J Long,
Therapist, Author, and Facilitator
The Gospel of Deliverance

INTRODUCTION

This book is a perspicacious theological perspective into the lifestyle and the call of the preacher. If you are a biblical analyst, it will challenge you at the very core of what you think about preaching and preachers.

Why is preaching necessary? Who really wants to hear about a God that they can't see with physical eyes? And how can a supernatural entity be displayed in a frail human vessel?

WHAT HAPPENED TO THE PREACHER: This is a thesis of convincing Grace, coupled with the recognition that God's preacher, at best, is a foolish personality wrapped in flesh, carnality, and promiscuity. Some prognosticators are incredibly narcissistic; other preachers are literally working sadistic immorality.

Some lecturers are engrossed with inversed humility. However, most who are preaching this ancient Jerusalem story TRULY LOVES THE LORD. Living their lives with ups and downs and changes and turns about.

A host of this prestigious army of Glory Criers is laboring under depression, suicidal thoughts, along grandiose ideas of greatness becoming icons in their generation. This book tapers to Jesus the Alpha and Omega, the King.

Now let us experience Him as the Beta King, the brightest star, and the diacritical responsive answer in the preacher's life.

ONE
"Behold the Lamb of God"

Can you feel the splash; can you see the waves on the lake rushing to the shore? Far beyond the Jordan River is a preacher whose swag is dressing in Camel's hair and eating bug protein sandwiches with a taste of wild honey. If you listen to him carefully, it sounds like he is cursing his church out down by the river. Can you imagine going to worship, and the pastor says, "you fornicators, you adulterers, you drunkards, you sons of whores." Indeed, this kind of preaching would cause the preacher to lose at least half, if not all, of his membership. Just because your great grandfather is Abraham causes you to think that you deserve this grace of baptism, splash splash?

"He said, I am the voice of one crying in the wilderness, Make straight the way of the Lord, as said the prophet Esaias."—John 1:23.

Straighten up your wicked thoughts; the Lord is coming, splash splash. Why don't you repent instead of showing up thinking just because you received this baptism, that will be enough for you? Repent for real and show authentic fruits, pure love, and a lifestyle change. Because you are really about to be cut-off from the top of your head to the root and the soil in which you claim to stand will never produce, and the church cried, "What will we do?" This old preacher, John the Baptist, an occupational baptizer, said, "as a mother would say to her children, share with your brothers who are in need."

Within a mind-shifting moment, John the Baptist becomes an accountant and says, "Stop cooking the books." Shifting so fast in his gift, he becomes an army commander, and he tells his soldiers to stop looting and be satisfied with their pay; work righteousness to get a promotion. The preacher's preacher John the Baptist.

John is poised; it is his time; it is his turn; it is his season! Let us put him on the billboard and put his pictures everywhere. And behold his swag; this preacher can curse you out and still baptize you. Man, who are you? You are definitely a boss in the Kingdom.

Look at how great your anointing is; you draw crowds in the wilderness. What do you have to say for yourself? "I Am the Voice," simply repeating Isaiah. Remove trickery and thoughts of deception from your heart, for the Lord is coming. So, stop looking at me like I am the Christ. I am not Him; however, I am His forerunner, His hype man.

"... but he will burn up the chaff with unquenchable fire."—Matthew 3:12.

"You snakes! You brood of vipers! How will you escape being condemned to hell?" —Matthew 23:33—NIV.

That is rough talk from a preacher; however, I submit to you this preaching saved souls and brought repentance to many.

The fame of this is far-reaching; he is known everywhere. The public believes he is sent from God; he is the savior in his day with the answers.

Behold the Lamb of God

He can be the Doctor Phil or the Oprah Winfrey of our day. Can't you hear them talk? Let us go see John the Baptist. He has Kingdom answers for us.

John minds his own business working in his assignment, which is to baptize in water and preach the coming of the Lord—one day, his destiny is fulfilled; "Behold the Lamb of God, which taketh away the sin of the world."—John 1:29.

There is no fanfare; there is no parade assembly. Instead, the Lamb of God steps through the crowd, and He is introduced and acknowledged by one of the greatest preachers in antiquity. John introduces the Jewish Rabbi everyone is looking for; His Name is Jesus.

The splashing stops; this loud-mouth preacher John the Baptist stops his sermon, which preachers seldom do. He doesn't say, "Hold on, wait one minute, I know there's a move of God, but I got to get my point across, and I really got a word."

However, this was not so with this great preacher John the baptizer. He stops his text, prevents the splashing, and is ready to perform the assignment he was sent on the earth to do, baptizing Christ Himself. The Word has shown up in the appearance of a man, a God-breathing man—Theos Pnosoks. This God-breathing man who needs no repentance of anything which has no sin type is requesting of John, "I would like to be baptized please."

A unique and exciting thing happened with these two cousin preachers. Standing by the river banks in front of the church, John and Jesus are debating who will baptize who. John had already told the church, "I am not worthy to stoop down and untie his shoes or even tie his shoes." And now Jesus has shown up, and John is saying, "I need you to baptize me." And Jesus is saying, "No, you're going to baptize me." I can almost hear the conversation between Jesus and John's family members arguing over church doctrine.

Finally, Jesus convinces John by using the word suffer it to be so, you're going to baptize me in this water. Needless to say, this preacher does something that most perhaps think they can grow out of; he respects the wishes of the pastor that ordained him from the foundation of the world.

What happened to these types of preachers, preachers who understand and hold you to the protocol of Kingdom way? Selah.

Two preachers, highly anointed, got the doctrine together right there at the river in front of the church, no arguing, no church splits; John baptizes Jesus.

Amid a baptismal service, the heavens began to open, and God the Father Himself begins to speak, applauding and celebrating His Son Jesus. God did not say, "Thank you, John, keep up the excellent work. He simply points to His Son and says, "This is My Beloved Son, and your actions today pleases me." I AM very excited about you, Son.

In my sanctified imagination, I can almost hear heaven saying, "all those that love you will follow you in this step that you have taken today."

What a blessing for the Church by the River to now follow the Lamb of God in baptism. By the way, John the Baptist will lose his mega-church today at the baptism service; however, he seems to have a good attitude about it.

What Happened to The Preacher

John the Baptist didn't do what most preachers would have done, stating, "I started this ministry down by the river, and this is my church, and if you don't like it, you can leave." This preacher clearly understands his mandate. It's not about him; it's about Jesus. John understands this so much that he literally told his followers and his disciples that he must decrease so that Jesus will increase.

John's church slowly fades away and begins to migrate into following Jesus. What happened to preachers like this that understand the mandate that the church belongs to Christ and the Kingdom belongs to God, and the Spirit of the Lord who descends is the ministering spirit in the sanctuary. Most preachers in modernity would literally go into a state of depression over losing their church to another preacher.

However, this is precisely what happened to John the Baptist when Jesus came on the scene, John's assignment was now completed, and John's time to shine ended, and the church folks won't be calling on him anymore. They will follow the One he just baptized and make no mistake; there is no comparison to teaching and preaching and theology; He is the God Preacher from Heaven.

Meanwhile, John the Baptist left the church service, goes home to his wilderness estate, and reflects on the superb baptism service they had that day; what a blessing. He baptized a tax accountant, a senator, Roman soldiers, and suddenly, the Lamb of God showed up; Jesus Himself to be baptized. Selah.

I can see him now kicking back, having a locust sandwich with a bit of honey butter, and drinking some grape wine, and then his space gets invaded and raided. I wonder if some of the very soldiers that were down at the baptismal service were present at this raid? They took him, binds him, and takes him to prison. What did this preacher prophet do? He goes from a great move of God to an open heaven experience and then to jail.

Really Lord?

I can hear the chatter now and the scuttlebutt! Did you hear about John the Baptist; he's in jail? What, in prison? What happened? I don't

What Happened to The Preacher

know. I heard he was walking around in that camel skirt. He was exposing himself to some of the sisters. He got arrested for indecent exposure. No, Sir, I heard he was drunk and got arrested for disorderly conduct. No, Sir, he was stealing church's money and calling us snakes to our faces trying to make us feel guilty. I knew there was something about him I just didn't like, but he could Preach!

Crowds would go down to his services and get baptized; however, once Jesus showed up, I don't even think people go out to his church anymore; they go over there to Jesus' ministry, and Jesus got a devil in charge of his bank account. These preachers, I don't know!

Listen, this is what I heard happened to John. King Herod invited a few of his senators and governors, and constituents to his house for a dine-in gathering and entertainment. That night they had a few strippers, and one of the strippers was King Herod's wife's daughter. What kind of mama would let her daughter strip for her husband; and his friends. Herodias is now Herod's wife. And John the Baptist is the kind of preacher that wasn't afraid of anything or afraid of anyone.

John the Baptist put King Herod on blast. He boldly told the king that it is unlawful for him to have his brother's wife! And this made Herodias (Herod's current wife) that used to be married to his brother, very upset. Salome, Herod's stepdaughter, turned up at the birthday party. Salome's mere presence made this old king get all hot and bothered, but he couldn't throw money at his step-daughter with his wife standing there. So he made an announcement by telling Salome, *"I'll give you whatever you want up to half of my kingdom if you dance for us."* I heard some of the other sisters at the church saying, *"I'll dance for the King."*

Salome is a young woman that doesn't know what she wants. So, she goes to her mother, Herodias, and asks, *"What shall I ask of the King?"* Herodias imparts a Jezebel spirit into her daughter, telling her to ask for the head of John the Baptist. Herodias inwardly said, *"I got that preacher, I got him!"*

The ministry of Jesus is doing fine. He is baptizing more people than John the Baptist. The fame of the ministry of Christ is going forward and doing exceptionally well. Entire cities are coming to Christ, people are getting healed, being set free, and the Word of God is being explained more perfectly because the WORD Himself has now been manifested in the earth.

That fiery baptizing preacher John has done an excellent and magnificent assignment for the Godhead; now he's in prison. What's interesting is that no lawyer has gone to see him. No one has paid his bail to get him out, and the one he halted his baptismal service for as John declared, Behold the Lamb of God who takes away the sins of the world.

Jesus did not even go and see John while he was in prison.

Oh, my God!!!

I know a church hurt is coming.

"He would not even come to see me in prison. All this preaching I have done in his name."

All these people are following Him because of me. I built this church, and He gets to walk in and takes it while I am in this jail, about to have my head cut off merely from preaching the truth. In walks, a millennial chick in antiquity and dances, and I lose my head,

Really God?

John sent for his disciples and gave them instructions to ask Jesus, "Are you the one who is to come, or should we expect someone else?" —Matthew 11:3—NIV. Is this how I am going to die after all I have done for you?

Jesus replies, "Go tell John blind people are seeing, lame people are walking, deaf people are hearing, I'm walking into funerals getting bodies out of caskets; the good news is being preached to the poor just like he did it before I arrived. Also, tell him that he is blessed because he is not offended over my work in the Lord." —Luke 7:22—NIV — paraphrased.

What Happened to The Preacher

'After John's messengers left, Jesus began to speak to the crowd about John: "What did you go out into the wilderness to see? A reed swayed by the wind?"'—Luke 7:24.

Tell my cousin goodbye I will see him later. There is none greater than John. A preacher's preacher embedded with Elijah's spirit, not interested in popularity, but interested in his assignment from heaven received while his father Zacharias was standing praying at the altar, conceived in Elizabeth's womb; there is no greater preacher before Jesus than John. —Luke 7:28-NIV-paraphrased.

Well done, John returns home. Don't forget the day you heard God say, "He was well pleased with me."

John had a hand in the pleasing!

TWO
"God's Business"

I heard the Voice of God when I was nine years old. I was sitting on the second row at the Kingsley Terrence Church of Christ in Indianapolis, Indiana, and I heard the Voice of God. I audibly heard God say, *"I am going to raise you amongst your brothers; some will love you, but most will hate you in this church denomination."*

At the age of nine, sister Lula would constantly prophesy to me every other Sunday. She would say, *"Son, you are going to preach."* I would look at her with great astonishment and amazement, thinking about the Voice that I would often hear telling me I would preach. Looking back on it all now, I chuckle because I realize, first of all, I am in the wrong church to even hear the Voice of God. This church does not believe in prophesying, nor do they believe that God speaks audibly through the Rhema

Word. They only believe in God's Logos (His Written Word). The Lord can speak past our denominational thoughts and our doctrinal thinking.

I would hear one elder say, *"everybody can't think in millions of dollars."* Church, this is God's Business, he would say. God's Business: I am nine years old. Sister Lula sitting two rows back, tells me every Sunday I am going to preach, and the elder stands up and says, this is God's Business, and I am sitting on the second row screaming within myself I am nine years old!

One Sunday school morning, my teacher taught us a lesson about Jesus when He was 12 years old. He was in a temple talking to doctors, lawyers, scribes, and Pharisees. But He was supposed to be on His way home with His parents. His parents thought that He was in the company of one of His family members as they were traveling together. Only to discover that Jesus was not present when they got home. Oh my God, they've lost the boy preacher. —Luke 2:44-45—paraphrased.

His parents returned to Jerusalem to find Him, and they found Jesus in the temple, sitting and talking to the doctors, both hearing them and asking them questions. His mother asked, "son why have you dealt with us this way?" You were lost, and we could not find you. —Luke 2:46-48 — paraphrased.

Jesus simply answered and said, "What do you mean you couldn't find me; do you not know I must be about my father's business?" —Luke 2:49 —paraphrased. God's Business.

I am nine years old, and I am ready to get about God's Business. I do not know what that entails; nevertheless, here I go. So, I started watching my preacher or pastor. I would listen carefully to something that he would preach, and then I would go back home, and I would preach it again to myself. I can still hear his booming voice in my spirit to this very day. Are you going to stand there and shake a fist of rebellion in the face of an almighty God, he would say at his close? (Repent for the time is at hand)—Matthew 3:2—repent that hell may not be your eternal home.

Oh yes, I got it now, God's Business is to tell the people to repent, and the time is at hand, lest hell be their eternal home. Fast forward to today's world at the beginning of this new decade, preachers do not even believe in hell anymore. Preachers do not believe that the earth is going to burn, and all things will be destroyed.

The grace message and the prosperity in abundance message have taken over the goodness of the Gospel. The Gospel of Grace has saved us from a burning hell; the Gospel of prosperity and abundance should keep us from living like hell.

Nevertheless, we are using Grace like a Maserati, and it seems okay to practice sin; Grace got it covered. Personally, I prefer the Rolls-Royce of Grace, and it is okay to live in great abundance and wealth that God's Business will procure for us. We can live any way we want to live; it is okay with God; Grace got it. Beloved, I believe it is dangerous to test the power of Grace constantly overtly. Death wins in Sin; Grace wins in Life.

If you cannot preach against sin, get out of God's Business. Grace saved Noah; however, sin destroyed Noah's world. God sent Christ into the world that He may destroy the works of darkness; Christ is triumphant over all sin, and He is the embodiment of Grace seated at the right hand of God, with all Authority of the Godhead. He has the rule over all principalities and power in high places and darkness. The uniqueness of God's Business is that God is like a master chess player. You can never checkmate the King of Heaven.

Church members will come and go. Men will get promoted to the Bishop and move into position themselves and to no avail save a cross around their neck with a belly full of iniquity. Rooks will Castle, and yet holiness still cannot abide in its wall. Queens will run astray with a Jezebel spirit, and knights will jest and fall. And the King will always be left standing victoriously.

When the preacher understands that their position is likened to a pawn on the master's chessboard, it will be easy to acknowledge and comprehend that you will be elevated in the world and promoted in the spirit realm. Nevertheless, you are for the Masters' use, and every position that God will shift you into is for His purpose and His glory and not our self-gain. However, Sonship has its privileges; it brings influence, social recognition, and perhaps a modicum of wealth; however, the preacher's mandate is still evident. "Sirs, we want to see Jesus."— John 12:21.

How can we manifest Jesus in this decade that begins with twenty-twenty? Prophetically, the prophets, the apostles, the pastors, and the teachers have been declaring its 20/20 vision. And rightly so, numerically, so. However, I submit to you another image, a vision that has seen the appearance of the Lord, and He is coming for a remnant. He is coming for a people, and He is coming for an ecclesia (His church), utterly void of any virus in its love festivals.

There are no schisms of racial inequality flowing in its veins: and every language declaring love and holiness is appreciated. Lord come quickly, He cried in His book. No one is asking Him to come; we are asking Him to save us from pestilence. We are asking Him to save us from an economic crisis. We are asking Him to forgive us of our sins and heal our bodies.

Yet We Are Not Asking Him (Lord Come Quickly!)—Revelation 20:20. This is how we manifest Jesus.

And for some, as you read this book, the Lord has come and taken some away.

And when the Lord shall return, it's God's Business only. What happened to you talking about this preacher? God is serious about His Business. So serious, I can recall the time when I got my first Love. It was a little country church in Moulton, Alabama. I remember people would say things like, *"Well, at least he's honest with God. And if he's going to do anything for the Lord, he's going to take it seriously, and he's not going to work halfhearted towards an assignment that the Lord has given him."*

They would say things like, *"He liked going to Tunica, Mississippi, to do a little gambling, eat a little food, hang out with his girlfriend. And he would be back Sunday morning on time for worship."* Pastor, at least I am honest with the Lord, and I will not play around with Him.

And some would say, *"I would fall out with great laughter and great reverence simultaneously; at least I am honest!"*

That's what you would tell the Lord?

It's okay; much grace will be applied. The Lord knows my heart. Being the classic bible thumper, I would quote scriptures like "The heart is deceitfully wicked who can know it, I the Lord try the reins of the heart."—Jeremiah 17:9.

With boldness and sarcasm, I would say,

"I, Lord, am honest too. I am going to hold to what I said honestly." They would go to the house of money, and I would still take their winnings in the offering plate. Also, I was reliably talking to DB (dope boy), taking his money like clockwork. Telling him it won't bless him, but it'll sure bless the Kingdom.

Really preacher?

What Happened to The Preacher

You see, this is God's Business, and the church got to stay functional.

The things we do as church leadership all in the name of God's work. Is making the announcement that God said, *"there is $100,000 in the room a good work?"* And is that God's Business, or is that just pastor needing $100,000, which is a total legitimate need for the kingdom's business? Is it God's Business to get a Rolls-Royce? Is it God's Business to get a Cessna 18 jet plane? Is it God's Business for me to have an entourage as protection that escorts me around as though I am the president? I do not see anything wrong with any of these examples. However, the question I would ask, is it God's Business? Or is it the preacher's business?

The Gospel needs a good-looking ticket, right?

Jesus rode in on a donkey never before ridden. (Luke 19:30-NIV). They held a parade for Him as He rode into the city-all praises to the King of the Jews. (John 12:13)—paraphrased.

So, what's wrong with the preacher flying in on his private jet? So, what's wrong with the preacher driving a Rolls-Royce? So, what's wrong with the preacher's wife having a Maserati? What's wrong with the preacher's kids having a Mercedes-Benz or a BMW driving them to school? I would suggest that there is absolutely nothing wrong with such luxuries.

However, if church members struggle to keep a roof over their head, pay bills such as light, water, etc., or struggle to keep a job, a few of them may be homeless. I would sell the private jet and take care of God's Business, His people. Right? Wrong!

How about we train God's people to be self-sufficient? And practice abundant giving in all things, and watch God give the increase.

Now, these scenarios can be very controversial for the preacher. The preacher looks like a *baller*. What happened to God's Business? The Bible says, "He that wins souls is wise."—Proverbs 11:30. Reaching the lost is what the heart of God wants more than anything.

A Soul Saving Business.

THREE
"Fresh Oil"

Turn to your neighbor, slap him high five and tell him it's your time. Spin around three times; tell your neighbor it's your turn. Run around the sanctuary tell your neighbor God is bringing you out of it. Yes, He may not come when *you* want Him, but He's always on time!

Jesus, Mary's baby. Jesus, rock in a weary land. Jesus, shelter in the time of a storm. Jesus, Moses burning bush on Fire. You do not have to wait until the battle is over to shout. **Shout Now!**

Do you get the idea? Taking clips and sound bites from others, and at some level, repetition really could be our best friend. However, Satan himself is not even afraid of the same Jesus clichés and watch phrases.

The devil is a lie! I hear Satan laughing every time I hear this phrase being used. Now it's a true statement; however, it's the same trick. We acknowledge more of a lying devil than we believe a triumphant Christ.

"It is a good thing to give thanks unto the Lord, and to sing praises unto thy name, O Most high: To shew forth lovingkindness in the morning, and thy faithfulness every night."—Psalms 92:1-2.

How is it that we start the day with a shallow thankfulness? Thank you, Lord. Hopping up out of bed and jumping in the shower. Quickly get dressed, out the door, instead of rising early and genuinely seeking the Lord for His wise counsel, wisdom, direction, protection, and prosperity for the day. Preacher, let us get back to giving the Lord thanks early in the morning. Let us offer our awake offering before we go into our plow field. And when we return from the day's journey, let us give our rest offering of thanksgiving. I believe this type of gratefulness will manifest the flow of Fresh Oil daily from the throne room of heaven. The Bible says, "...there is nothing new under the sun."—Ecclesiastes 1:9b—NIV.

We can coin a new watch phrase:

The Triumphant Jesus! And receive fresh Revelation concerning the dispensation in the time in which we now live.

How do we stay relevant in a world where the Gospel has been turned into a Glamspel. Or now it's gospel-licious, gospel-cinematic, gospel music, and gospel-millennials. And yet, the Lord has commanded us:

"Go ye therefore, and teach all nations, baptizing them in the name of the Father, and of the Son, and of the Holy Ghost: Teaching them to observe all things whatsoever I have commanded you: and, lo, I am with you always, even unto the end of the world. Amen."—Matthew 28:19-20.

However, instead of the church teaching the world, it seems that the world is guiding the church. I do not wish to be harsh to the church because God loves the church, and God loves the world. So, preacher, are we looking for a world that looks like the church? Or are we looking for a church that looks like the world? God loves both. Jesus said, "even unto the end of the world." —Matthew 28:20.

Here is a biblical deliverance, the Apostle Peter is an older man now. I suppose now and then he might slip and say a few cuss words. And if you cross him the wrong way, he might stab you. Nevertheless, he's now a seasoned Apostle. He explains in his narrative derived from divine inspiration, a form of deliverance that we often do not pay attention to; however, one thing is correct; God delivers. Talk Peter!

"For if God did not spare angels when they sinned, but sent them to hell, putting them in chains of darkness to be held for judgement; and if he rescued Lot, a righteous man, who was distressed by the depraved conduct of the lawless." —2 Peter 2:4,7—NIV.

Only eight persons saved in the Old World (Noah the preacher of righteousness) —2 Peter 2:5 and his family, Noah's world has ended. Lot living a vexed lifestyle over in Sodom and Gomorrah. Lot's world has ended with hellfire and brimstone. I ponder what Noah was saying; what was his text? Did he sledgehammer and talk at the same time? Did he tell them that babies were going to drown? Did he tell them that their dead carcasses would be slamming against the ark?

Did he tell them that drowning would close their vocal cords, and they could not even scream for help from the Lord? Did he tell them the very breath of God would leave their bodies? Did he tell them that when the water fills their lungs that their hearts would stop? Did he fully explain to them that the ark was a place of Grace and safety?

He preached the same message for 120 years. It is going to rain. I am pretty sure they got bored with his sermon. Nevertheless, can you see Noah (instant in season and out of season) —2 Timothy 4:2?

Preach preacher! Nobody wants to talk about hellfire today. Just tell us smooth things, preacher. (They say to the seers, see no more visions. And to the prophets, give us no more visions of what is right. Tell us pleasant things, prophesy illusions.) —Isaiah 30:10—NIV.

"Therefore, hell has enlarged herself and open her mouth without measure: and their glory, and their multitude, and their pomp, and he that rejoiceth, shall descend into it. And the mean man shall be brought down, and the mighty man shall be humbled: and the eyes of the lofty shall be humbled; But the Lord of hosts shall be exalted in judgment, and God that is holy shall be sanctified in righteousness." —Isaiah 5:14-16. —paraphrased.

Hell is real, and somebody is going; I just don't want it to be me, and I don't want it to be you.

Beloved, I would not have a preacher that could not preach the Hell out of me or have a preacher that would not teach me the Grace of God as His teaching removes me from the shores of Hell's fire. (Hell has enlarged herself) —Isaiah 5:14. Interesting, why does the Bible describe Hell as a female?

Now, I do not wish to be misogynistic; however, I believe that the Holy Spirit describes Hell as *her* simply due to Hell's deceptive nature. I carefully attributed this to the Holy Spirit because it is in the holy writ (Hell has enlarged herself) —Isaiah 5:14, and He does not waste words. Please also note that the Holy Spirit also describes Wisdom as (Her). If you are a biblical analyst, you would have discovered this in the proverbial writings.

We see a (Her) personality specifically categorized as Wisdom in one setting and Hell in another. "Say to the [skillful and godly] wisdom, "You are my sister," And regarding understanding and intelligent insight as to your intimate friends; That they may keep you from the immoral woman, From the foreigner [who does not observe God's laws and] who flatters with her [smooth] words." —Proverbs 7:4-5— AMP.

It is here we understand that Wisdom has a deceptive sister. And that deceitful sister is described in Proverbs —7:27— "Her house is the way to hell, going down to the chambers of death." In this verse, she is the grave, described as stubborn, turbulent, prideful, and strong-willed. This is the deceptive personality of Wisdom's demonic sister.

However, Wisdom's personality operating by holiness stands with the Lord. In Proverbs 8:22, she [Wisdom] is the Lord's personal possession. "The Lord possessed me in the beginning of his way before his works of old."

Every time we speak of Jehovah, we must talk about (her) Wisdom. She tells us, (then I

Wisdom was beside Him as a master and director of the work, and I was daily and his delight, rejoicing before Him always.)-Proverbs 8:30—AMP. Wisdom's deceptive sister presents herself as truth; however, she is a false light. And she gives us the perception that Hell is not real. Let's call her (Sheimsheir)[1]—at the writing of this book, this name does not exist on planet earth yet; her spirit of deception runs rampant.

No one wants to hear a constant repent or go to hell message. I do admit that as the preacher, perhaps we have packaged the message wrong. The Hellfire message seems to be constant doom and gloom. No one wants to hear, "make sure you have your hellfire insurance message." It is amazing; we keep our car insurance paid and our homeowner's insurance paid. We even plan for our burials to be paid. And yet, we have no desire to look over our Grace policy, ensuring it is updated when we have an enemy seeking to kill, steal, and destroy our lives in the human form (Sheimshier).

---

[1] Phonetically prounced she-him-he-is-her like as in she's him/he's her.

What Happened to The Preacher

How do we keep a Fresh Oil word amid a world with stale ears, blurred eyes, and artificial minds? Preacher! We tell him Hell is hot! And the fire is never quenched. We tell them, "Hell is hotter than baby girl," dancing on a stripper pole. We tell them Hell is hotter than a baller's billiards where the stakes are high. So preacher man, when you do not have a new word and cannot make those leftovers taste fresh in your pericope, you should consider, have you been hanging out with (Sheimshier), Wisdom's demonic sister?

She is deceptive in all of her ways. She has an allure of truth. She is a residue of her Queen Mother Lilith and her Grandmother Jezebel and her Aunt Athaliah, a personification of Hell. Pastors, teachers, apostles, bishops, and deacons are currently lying in the bed of adultery, an affliction with Wisdom's demonic sister. Her deception does not stop in the kingdom—her deception reins in political arenas. There is no function that she will not attend.

Sheimshier is Satan's concubine, and her spirit is strategically staged against truth and holiness.

She is the root cause of houses that continued with the spirit of "a fretting leprosy."—Leviticus 13:51-52. And wherever she is and whoever she is with, drama and chaos never cease to follow her.

Nevertheless, she cannot remain in the house of Fresh Oil. She can undoubtedly visit and cast her demonic spell coupled with a web of deception. She cannot stay in the home where the man of God has a prayer life. Her feet will not stay in the way of righteousness. The Fresh Oil of the word of the Lord paints a picture of her true deception in her own face.

Her counteraction against God's word is to adorn herself with dead hair, false eyes, fake breasts, fake buttocks, fake fingernails. And then parade in the presence of the Lord, as though she is holy. However, the Fresh Oil of the word of the Lord burns her flesh and exposes her lewdness.

On the other hand, her counterpart lover is full of crookedness, pornography, and perversion. He is a stalker who preys on innocent ones. He is well-dressed well versed in languages. He is an ambassador of the antichrist. He takes bribes and steals from the treasury in the house of the Lord. He is a male whore, and his lips are full of the butter-mouth[2] spirit.

Nevertheless, the Fresh Oil of the word of the Lord will destroy him.

Preacher, why are we so comfortable cohabitating with this spiritual androgyny? Selah

---

[2] Reference Psalms 52:21.

FOUR
"Old School"

Man, did you smell alcohol on the pastor's breath? Did you see the pack of Salem lights in his front shirt pocket? No, Sir, the pastor smokes Cuban cigars. He drinks a little Hennessy, and he likes to play spades on Thursday nights. Unbelievable, a man with such worldly profligacy, can preach the Hell out of you on Sunday morning and have you crying, scared that if we do not repent, the Lord will send us to Hell. Needless to say, the first lady is gorgeous; however, the preacher's car is parked at sister Mae-Mae's house.

Now, do not go starting rumors. Sister Mae-Mae is the church secretary, and the pastor needs to get some extra work done before Sunday morning. It's all right, Amen. Sister Mae-Mae and the pastor have been working like this for years, and as long as the first lady has nothing to say about it, you should not gossip about it. Lord Jesus, it is Sunday morning, and I was working my Sunday morning paper route around 6:00 a.m., and I saw the preacher coming out of sister Mae-Mae's house at 6:30 a.m. Unbelievable dedication working all night to get the church bulletin together for Sunday Morning. What a blessing! It is 11:45 a.m., and Praise and Worship are now over.

The preacher is in the pulpit, and he is boiling his water. Church, indeed God has been kind to us, God has looked down through the corridors of time and called our souls, and He has called us to this moment of worship, and we are grateful to Him for He has extended the briskly threads of our lives and He's allowed our golden moments to roll on a little further.

God allowed us to rise this morning early; I wish I had some help in here. "Did sister Mae-Mae help you up this morning, preacher?" Beloved, if you will tarry with me, the preacher man will be here in a little while.

Nevertheless, we give a gracious welcome to the Holy Spirit in this sanctuary that He can have His way and move and speak and interrupt and change the service if He so pleases. "Say it, Doc!" Hasn't God been good to you, Church? "Amen, let the redeemed of the Lord say so."—Psalms 107:2. Beloved, if you will meet me on Hallelujah Boulevard and walk down Praise Alley with me, we will jog over to Glory Park together, and when we get there, we will dance around the fountain of Life. I wish I had a praying Church!

Beloved, there is a word from the Lord. You all going to talk to me. Turn in your Bibles... Hold up, sister Mae-Mae has started to shout, and the pastor has not even given the text. Oh, that's right, she already has the memo. Go ahead, and sister Mae-Mae get your Shout Out! It is obvious now that the preacher was not doing anything at 4:00 a.m. this morning. He continues to say, Beloved, if you have your copy, turn with me to Luke Chapter 10, beginning at verse 17-20— "And the seventy returned again with Joy, saying, Lord, even the devils are subject unto us through thy name."

"And he said unto them, I beheld satan as lightning fall from heaven." —verse 18.

"Behold, I give unto you power to tread on serpents and scorpions, and over all the power of the enemy: and nothing shall by any means hurt you." —verse 19.

"Notwithstanding in this rejoice not, that the spirits are subject unto you; but rather rejoice, because your names are written in heaven." —verse 20.

Please take note that the seventy did not return telling Jesus that the devil is a lie. They told the Lord, (...demons submit to your name) —Luke 10:17—NIV.

Interestingly, the Lord admonishes them not to be so impressed with bringing demons into subjection. In other words, they were not demon chasers. Their assignment was to (heal the sick, and tell them that the kingdom of God has come to you.) —Luke 10:9—paraphrased. Even Jesus Himself never chased demons; however, demons tend to manifest themselves when Jesus would enter into the synagogue or the landscape.

What I reflect on as I ponder the Old School preacher's life, he did not consider himself to be more than he was. He did not put on a front as though he had all power in his hands, like some of us so-called apostles, prophets, pastors, and teachers. The preacher was a natural man, and *supernatural* oil would pour from his pericope when he would mount the ecclesiastical desk on a Sunday morning.

He might even shout Lord have mercy while he was preaching. And you would think he's shouting over how good God is. However, he is shouting because the sister in the yellow dress is taking her seat. And her hips are swaying to the (Lord is my shepherd) —Psalms 23:1. I see what I want! I wish to reiterate I take no slight at the anointed apostle, prophet, pastor, or teacher.

However, I call into question the entitlement system, the spiritual extortion, though some abused these offices, designed for the spiritual edification of the body of Christ. The Apostle Paul seems to have a sexual sin struggle. The Prophet Elijah killed 450 false prophets and turned and ran from one woman, Jezebel. Pastors are not studying the word; anything goes; dressed fly while teaching so the audience can admire their clothes more than the word.

However, Old School preacher would walk in sporting his brim hat, cape, and if you weren't careful, he had a cane and his Bible in his hand. Old School preacher, no armor-bearer needed. Old School preacher would not let you touch his Bible; his Bible was like his gun, untouchable.

Modern-day apostles are promiscuous with their Bibles. Prophets would rather make a profit than prophesy the truth to power. Pastors (spend most of their time chasing women and drinking) — the Temptations 1972. And teachers wish to hear titillating things, as opposed to tow the "line-up on-line and precept upon precept here a little there a little."—Isaiah 28:10.

The Old School preacher would tell it like IT IS! Not afraid to lose his job and look you in your face and tell you he will add more to it before taking anything away from what he preached. Turn to his wife and say, baby, let's go. You drive, get in his car, light his cigar, and drive off. Stop by the bootleg house, pick up his bottle of Brandy, go home, and have his dinner. And afterward, if he felt like it, make love to his wife, hold her in his arms, and go to sleep.

Old School message to the reader, I hear you. It sounds like this preacher is not saved.

However, I submit to you that this is what the Old School preachers taught millennials to practice. That Old School preacher preaching--repentance, fire, and brimstone saved my soul. Nevertheless, it caused many boomers to be immersed in religious doctrines; at best, they are doctrines of Satan. If you don't worship like me, you are going to Hell. If you do not practice holiness, you are going to Hell.

This is probably the truth; however, the Apostle Paul was the crowned apostle of grace as radical as it seems. (But by the grace of God, I am what I am: and his grace to me was not without effect. No, I worked harder than all of them--yet not I, but the grace of God that was with me.) —I Corinthians 15:10—paraphrased, this is good shouting ground. The Apostle Paul becomes one with the grace given unto him even though he is still in his physical flesh with all of his profligacies

When this preacher of Judaism becomes ordained by Apostolic Grace, he is transformed into the I AM of God. I hear Paul saying, (I wasted the church)—Galatians 1:13.

Old School

"I stood by and watched Stephen die."—Acts 22:20. I held their clothes on layaway while they killed this young man. And the same people that killed him turned around and beat me. All because I am infused with the grace that I once denied and detested and rejected.

Beloved, all your Old School preacher did was sleep with sister Mae-Mae. Get him a little drink on Thursday, and study the Bible while he would take a small sip. This shows us the Old School God. He loves us so much and can find Grace in anyone Noah, Moses, David, Samson, Paul, and the Old School preacher.

FIVE
"Suicide"

And it came to pass, when she pressed him daily with her words, she urged him, so that his soul was vexed unto death.—Judges 16:16.

She begged for his strength; what happens to the preacher when life yearns for his strength? Samson, affectionately known as Mr. Sunshine, has great strength, power, and great weakness. His physical prowess rivals the strength of Superman and all of the marvel superheroes. This superhuman could defeat armies with his bare hands. Nevertheless, his Achilles heel seems to be swaying hips, a diamond in the belly button, feet that smell like frankincense and myrrh, and a nice weave with sexy tattooed breasts.

The softness of her voice, her breast milk made for man's taste, the tattoos are inked on her back at the top of her buttocks. The way she coaches him into her lap, to drink of her nectar.

Suicide

The treacherous threesome, which leads to a haircut, and his strength is gone.

"And she made him sleep upon her knees; she called for a man, and she caused him to shave off seven locks of his head; and she began to afflict him, and his strength went from him." —Judges 16:19.

Wake up preacher from your sleep; how is it that she can afflict you, and you don't know it. The dinner was lovely; the wine was fine, the ambiance and the setting were highly seductive. How is it, preacher, that you didn't realize that this sexy kryptonite would make you commit suicide? Surely she loves me. She loves bombs me all day. She tells me she misses me. She tells me she wants me. She tells me she can't live without me. Why would I lie to her about my secrets? She's my ride and die.

"And she said, The Philistines be upon thee, Samson. And he awoke out of his sleep, and said, I will go out as at all other times before, and shake myself. And he wist not that the Lord was departed from him." —Judges 16:20.

How is it man of God that you did not recognize that the Lord Himself had departed from you? As we can clearly see, it's a suicide mission. "Our God has delivered Samson our enemy into our hands." —Judges 16:23.

All this time, Delilah was Dagon's woman. Dagon, half fish, half-man. A fertility demon. A day walking vampire spirit deity. Just think Samson could have found a woman in Israel and had superhuman children. Nevertheless, he is overcome by strange flesh.

That literally cost him his ministry. But by the grace of God, he is recorded in the Hebrew Hall of Fame. —Hebrews 11:32.

Now he is in the grind of his life, literally. Grinding as an ox shredding out wheat, his very strength, his same anointing, is now being made a mockery by his captors.

Needless to say, his enemy did not understand that to touch God's anointing is also a suicide mission. His enemies are now having a party; we got him; we have the super Samson!

The Philistines strippers are dancing. Delilah has now been promoted by the Holy Spirit as she will forever be known as a temptress that seduced and tricked Mr. Sunshine, AKA Samson. Preacher, you better beware of when she says, *"Good morning sunshine,"* it may cause you to commit suicide. The Holy Spirit decided that He would not allow us to forget that this woman Delilah is Dagon's Harlot. Selah.

In my sanctified imagination, in the similitude, Jesus Christ appears as a little lad and leads the wounded warrior into the den of mockery. Samson is still of the order that he is God's anointed, called to defeat the Philistines, and requests the little lad. He exclaims to him that he is tired, he makes a request of the lad to allow him to rest against the pillows.

'Then Samson said to the lad who held him by the hand, "Let me feel the pillars which support the temple, so that I can lean on them."' —Judges 16:26-NKJV.

The obedience of the lad is incredible. He does not take him astray; he does precisely what Samson requires of him. While the Philistines are partying on their top platform, Samson is grinding on his platform below. Preacher, it doesn't matter what level you are on; God has a plan and a purpose for your assignment, whether it be the top platform or the bottom platform. Samson's platform is to destroy the Philistines. Man of God, your platform is to continue to push back against the works of darkness and declare the Triumphant Jesus.

"My son, keep my words, and lay up my commandment with thee." —Proverbs 7:1.

"That they may keep thee from the strange woman, from the stranger with flattereth with her words." —Proverbs 7:5.

"So she caught him, and kissed him, and with an impudent face said unto him, I have peace offerings with me, this day I have payed my vows." —Proverbs 7:13-14.

"Come, let us take our fill of love until morning: let us solace ourselves with loves. For the goodman is not at home, he is gone a long journey: He hath taken a bag of money with him, and will come home at the day appointed." —Proverbs 17:18-20.

Preacher, a jealous man, can't work. However, as you can see, her husband had no problem with doing what he had to do to provide for his wife and family.

Unfortunately for marriages that are in a suicide watch, a man must decide what type of man he will be. He must decide if he's going to be a hard-working man or a broke man. Unfaithful relationships can cause suicide. My son, hear my words, *"if her husband leaves her at home and takes some money with him, trust me, you can leave her alone as well."*

"She caught him with a kiss." —Proverbs 7:13. She told him she was married. What are you thinking, preacher? Is she really worth it? She has cast down many wounded; yea, many strong men have been slain by her.

"Her house is the way to hell, going down to the chambers of death." —Proverbs 7: 27.

She is not your intimate friend; she is not understanding. She is too emotional, suffering from a borderline personality disorder, which is literally why her husband can stay away from her for long periods. Work a double, work on holidays, and work the third shift because he has no desire to be in a cantankerous house.

Nevertheless, you, foolish young preacher (void in your understanding) —Proverbs 7:7, you literally think you can defeat this stubborn temptress by humbling her in her husband's bed-chamber. And your Father has clearly warned you. Your Father, the King, is adored by thousands of women. And yet, He's King because He would never succumb to such treachery and deception; in His household or His Kingdom. Preacher, I would like to tell you, do not sleep with the women in your church or mess with the church's money; it is suicide.

There is no recovery from spiritual suicide. The travesty about suicide is that it is the individual's choice not to consider that the Heavenly Father always has more options than self-murder, whether spiritual or physical. The truth of the matter is that suicide has been around since the garden of Eden. Satan committed murder, Eve was tricked; however, Adam committed suicide.

"I have sinned in that I have betrayed the innocent blood. And they said, What is that to us? See thou to that. And he cast down the pieces of silver in the temple, and departed, and went and hanged himself."—Matthew 27:4-5.

Apostle Judas, the treasurer, I like to be very careful as I talk about this preacher apostle's ministry. Who handled the money in Jesus' ministry. Have we misapplied the grace of God concerning his life? The thought is very challenging. Seeing that the Lord told Peter, "Get thee behind me satan." —Matthew 16:23. And then Jesus says, "have I not chosen you and one of you is a devil." —John 6:70.

As I recall the final Passover, the master teacher is in the room with His disciples, His future apostles. He tells them at the Passover meal that one of them will betray him.

"And they began to be sorrowful, and to say unto him one by one, Is it I? and another said, Is it I?" —Mark 14:19. Judas betrays; however, Peter denies. And both of them have an opportunity of repentance. "And the Lord said, Simon, Simon, behold, Satan hath desired to have you, that he may sift you as wheat: But I have prayed for thee, that thy faith fail not: and when thou art converted, strengthen thy brethren." —Luke 22:31-32.

It is a strong possibility that Peter as well could be the potential betrayer. However, the master prayed for him. And preacher, Jesus never fails. However, on the other hand, we see Judas Iscariot. "And after the sop, Satan entered him. And Jesus said unto him do what you must do quickly." —John 13:27—paraphrased. Preacher, Judas could have been saved.

"Now no man at the table knew for what intent he spake this unto him." —John 13:28.

How is it, preacher, that you are sitting at the love feasts and unaware of what the master is saying to your ministry partners? Needless to say, men and women are sitting at your table, and make no mistake, some of them will betray you. Just pray that a maneuver will be swift that you may get on the other side of the embarrassment. Don't allow the betrayal to make you commit suicide. Don't let the scandal put you out of the ministry. Truth be told, every ministry needs a good scandal. "They meant it for evil, but God turned it to good."—Genesis 50:20-paraphrased. God weaved it, good.

Suicide

Preacher, don't kill yourself. If the doctor walks in the room and tells you, you only have 6 months to live. Don't kill yourself. Just say it is Christ who lives in me. Preacher, don't kill yourself. If you're married and your wife walks out on you. Remember Ezekiel? God gave his wife a stroke. And God told him He was going to do it.

"Son of man, behold, I take away from thee the desire of thine eyes with a stroke: yet neither shalt thou nor weep, neither shall thy tears run down. Forbear to cry, make no mourning for the dead, bind the tire of thine head upon thee, and put on thy shoes upon thy feet, and cover not thy lips, and eat not the bread of men."—Ezekiel 24:16-17.

Preacher, that can put you in an actual state of depression. "Remember Lot's wife."—Luke 17:32. Take a break, then after a while, plow on. Preacher, if you're fired from your church, just remember no man ever had a ministry for you anyway it was God who called you.

Woman of God, remember Nabal; he's a fool just as his name suggests. "...Nabal is his name, and folly is with him:"—1 Samuel 25:25. Preacher, whatever you do, don't commit suicide. Live preacher, Love preacher, Laugh preacher. (Ask the Savior to help you, comfort, strengthen, and keep you, He is willing to aid you. He will carry you through.) (Sacred hymn-Yield Not to Temptation). H.R. Palmer 1868. Preach the Hell out of yourself, and be Saved.

SIX
"What's with the Black Preacher?"

I remember it so vividly living in Decatur, Alabama, while in my second year of Bible College. A young man from Pakistan also attended the same class, The Fundamentals of Preaching. As we were sitting in class that day, this young man from Pakistan would ask the question, and I still grapple with it 25 years later. What's with the black preacher? He would ask. Of course, I did not say a word; I remained quiet to hear his comments.

"They wear hats, and they walk in with canes. They wear big cufflinks on their shirts, and they wear fancy outlandish shoes. They wear hip-hop gear to class." I chuckled. "And then, finally, they look like pimps instead of preachers."

I smiled, realizing that I was a dark-tone Christ Man[3] (Black Man) in the class.

All the focus suddenly shifted on me as I admired my beautiful Goldwing silver dollar size cufflinks. And, of course, I wanted to quote the scripture from the Apostle Paul.

"I have become all things to all people so that by all possible means I might save some this I do for the sake of the Gospel that I might share in its blessings."—1 Corinthians 9 22:23—NIV.

That's what I wanted to say, and it was indeed what I was thinking. However, what came out of my mouth was extremely shocking.

I began to speak with an impish grin upon my face telling the young man from Pakistan that his comments were well noted. Mostly, while he and his skin hue were one shade darker than mine. I publicly told him that it was very white of him to think that he can make such a comment amongst (Christ Men) (White Men) just to feel accepted and approved. I ended the dialog by saying, "that was very white of you," and

---

[3] Hear this phrase from Apostle Leroy Thompson.

you will soon discover you are not as privileged as you think you are in this conservative southern denominational Bible College.

However, you would think the dialogue would have ended when another student (Christ Man) (White Man) began to speak and say yes. "Why do they (Christ Man) (Black Man) shout and scream when they preach? What is that all about?"

I nearly fell out of my seat with extreme laughter, in my spiritual racism, stating that they do not have the Holy Spirit and are not saved. Not only that, I just turned in a paper on the Cultural Church emphasizing that the Caucasian American Church has a superiority complex against all non-Anglo-Saxon churches. Here I am in Bible College, and I am on my way to the president's office.

"George, the college president, asked, "Are you going to be a good boy?"

"Boy!!!"

I screamed in my spirit while smiling at my college president, who I really admired, and I admire him to this very day. I took a deep breath and simply said, Yes, Sir.

A few professors caught wind of what happened in the classroom and my excursion to the president's office. Four professors got in touch with me that week. I was badgered by two of them, who deliberately flunked me in their classes. One pulled me in the office told me he would fail me, so get ready to repeat the course because it is required for graduation. He cited that I thought I was smarter than he. And he told me I was not in Bible College to teach him. However, I was in biblical academia to be taught.

The other professor just flunked me and told me I would never be a great preacher. And that I would never preach in Leoma, Tennessee. However, two other professors really encouraged me. Admonishing me to be quiet, learn, get the main thing, graduate, and leave. It was quite an experience, needless to say.

I attended for three and a half years, and I did not graduate from that Bible College. I went on to some other school for preaching. Thus, because of my Bible institutions preaching experience in pastoral biblical knowledge, I was accepted into the Master of Divinity Program. I am currently in my Doctoral program. I have been learning for over 30 years.

The word of God is vast and wealthy with unfathomable truths. "I am not asking that you take them out of the world, but you keep them safe from the evil one; they do not belong in this world any more than I do."—John 17:15-16—NLT.

As my mind wanders back to the classroom, rethinking the Pakistan (Christ Man) statement, I realize that perhaps I had some worldly residue on my life that certainly made my appearance not look like a preacher.

And what does a preacher look like? I didn't sport camel hair, and I didn't have a long beard. But I did have some blinging cufflinks and a diamond ring. And yes, my shoes were boss.

Also, there were days I would sit back in a chair, cross my legs with such arrogance, lift my pants leg, and expose my socks, thinking that some female would find that attractive.

Yes, I think brother Pakistan could have been on to something. That's just speaking of myself, not other fine pontificators. However, no one has a right to judge any person based on how they look or dress. Nevertheless, my dress code betrayed my spiritual oil. Notwithstanding, I looked like what the rapper said in his song PIMP. I talked like a preacher, but my swag said to play a player instead of preaching the word.

This residue's struggle has been with me for a long time, I believe, perhaps all of my life. I loved fashion, and I like my fine style of hair. I like my designer clothes, and I like my fly shoes. I love seeing a woman in a sexy pair of shoes. Lord God, help us or help me; it's worldliness.

The old pioneer preacher wore suits every day. Oh, don't be deceived; he may have had his profligacy; nevertheless, when he walked into the room, you knew he was a preacher. Fast forward amidst a world such as today, the oil of God seems foreign. I see plenty of brother preachers preaching the word; however, it appears they just left GGs.

I see beautiful soul sisters preaching, and it looks like they just left GGs. This word of God has to be preached, and I believe we are just going to have to get over how God may present the package.

For it is written, I will destroy the wisdom of the wise, the intelligent of the intelligent, I will frustrate. Where is the wise person, where is the wise teacher of the law? Where is the philosopher of this age? Has God not made the foolish the wisdom of the world? For since in the wisdom of God, the world through its wisdom did not know Him, God was pleased through the foolishness of what was preached to save those who believe.—1 Corinthians 1:19-21—NIV.

What's up with the black preacher? There isn't a man on the planet that works so hard and looks so good and dresses so fine, and when he opens his mouth, you hear the oracles of God flow; Preach Christ, Man.

So if wearing silver dollar cufflinks offend you, I won't wear them anymore. If my ripped jeans make you feel a certain kind of way, I won't wear them anymore. If my shoes are too distracting for you, I will get a plain shoe. If my hairstyle is a distraction, pray with me, and I will pray with you. And I will probably go get a haircut.

Soul sister, if your dress is too tight, baby, you may be preaching; the oil and the fire are falling. However, every now and then, I am checking out your curves. And then I am going back to Shouting, and then I will repent for checking out your curves while God used you in such a mighty way. Preach, Christ woman.

My holiness must outlast my swag.

My righteousness must outlast my riffs.

My perfection must outlast my rejection.

My supplications must outlast my sensuality.

My long-suffering must outlast aloofness.

My love must outlast my life.

My joy must outlast my injustices.

My peace must outlast my pain.

My patience must outlast my pride.

My kindness must outlast my bitterness.

My goodness must outlast my deceitfulness.

My faithfulness must outlast my unfaithfulness.

My gentleness must outlast my conceit.

My self-control must outlast my in contingency.

What's up (Christ Man), Black Man?

Let's Pray.

SEVEN
"When Humility Kissed Holiness"

It was the summer of 1970; I was 7 years old. We were headed back home to Indianapolis, Indiana, leaving the town of Pickens, Mississippi. My mother was a member of the Kingsley Terrance Church of Christ in Indianapolis, Indiana. I will never forget the enthusiasm of my mother's faith in Christ Jesus. It is because of my mother and grandmother that I even know the name Jesus Christ. It was Sunday morning we were headed home. My mother wanted to worship; we stopped in a little town called Durant, Mississippi, and attended the Church of Christ there. As my mother walked in, she was greeted by one of the elders of the church.

He was not rude to her; he was actually very kind-hearted. Nevertheless, he stopped my mother in the building's foyer and expressed that this was an all-white congregation and no black people attended the church and politely asked her to leave. In humility, my mother stated that she was a member of the Church of Christ, and she was headed home to Indianapolis, Indiana, and she decided to stop in to worship, and she was not leaving.

I remember this encounter so vividly. I was silently standing next to my mother as all of this was unfolding. She expressed that she was not leaving with her face humbly looking toward the floor while repeating, *"All I want to do is worship."*

Quietly we entered the sanctuary, and we were seated on the very back row. Many years have passed, and I do not remember the songs sung or remember the sermon preached on that day. However, I remember it was communion service, and a young man, probably a deacon, came up to my mother with tears in his eyes. He stated that he was instructed that some local men would blow the church up if he served us communion. With tears in his eyes, he served my mother. My mother took the bread and wine, and we left the service. I often revisited this event's memory, and I ask myself the question, was this a true Church of God?

As I reflect on the times, my mother and I discussed this traumatic event, which has shaped my theology to this moment, I cannot help but remember my mother's demeanor.

When she talks of this story, she tells me how she had feared for her five little babies with her that Sunday in the house of the Lord. That day I discovered that some churches in America were attended by monsters. I also watched when my mother's Humility Kissed the Holiness of God. *"I just want to worship, she said, and we will leave."*

Christ is not in brick and mortar. Christ is not in a name registered on the outside of one's billboard or church building. Christ is in you. Christ's consciousness is the truth that must be established in the hearts of men.

"For this is the covenant that I will make with the house of Israel after those days, saith the Lord; I will put my laws into their minds, and write them on their hearts: and I will be to them a God, and they shall be to me a people." —Hebrews 8:10.

There is no doubt in my mind that the Holiness of God covered that little church in Durant,

Mississippi. An all-white congregation survived the humility of a few black souls.

"Follow peace with all men, and Holiness, without which no man shall see the Lord." —Hebrews 12:14.

I also remember the tears as they swelled up in my mother's eyes as she took the Lord's supper. I am thinking, is this the church Jesus died for so my mother can come to it and be treated like this?

"Mercy and truth are met together; righteousness and peace have kissed each other. Truth shall spring out of the earth, and righteousness shall look down from heaven."—Psalms 85:10-11.

"The fool hath said in his heart, There is no God. They are corrupt, they have done abominable works, there is none that doeth good. The Lord look down from heaven upon the children of men, to see if there were any that did understand, and seek God."—Psalms 14:1.

When we seek God, we are seeking the essence of true Holiness. If any man is longing for his first encounter with Jehovah Adonai, the

Sovereign One, he must first come face-to-face with His Holiness.

Look at the humility of God to scoop His hands down in clay. The beauty of the clay is the interaction that God has with it. "The humility of Holiness to touch the dirt and Create."

His Holiness that He would wrap Himself within His own Creation and then establish a permanent seal within it.

That He, God Himself, cannot escape nor will He ever abandon His Creation. "For God so loved the world, that he gave his only begotten Son, that whosoever believeth in him should not perish, but have everlasting life."—John 3:16.

Holiness is declared when the foundations of the earth were laid. This loving, kind Heavenly Birther humbled Himself. And calling forth sons and daughters, knowing that we would disobey Him. "Placed us in the boundary of our habitats." —Acts 17:26—paraphrased.

He gave us different languages, whereby those who seek humility and holiness will seek oneness in Him that we will be understood in our communication with each other as the sons of the living God. Living in our eternal priesthood, sharing Glory and the full essence of God's nature, becoming as God likewise.

Let Christ Himself be your example as to what your attitude should be. "For he, who had always been God by nature, did not claim to His prerogatives as God's equal, but stripped Himself of all of His privileges consenting to be a slave by nature and being born as a mortal man. And, having become a man, He humbled Himself by living a life of utter obedience, even to the extent of dying. And the death He died was the death of a common criminal. That is why God has now lifted Him so high."—Phillip Translation—2:6.

Humility has become intimate with Holiness. Holiness commands the repudiation of disgraceful deeds. Humility stands in the gap, preventing Holiness from destroying everything in its wake; this is truly a paradoxical circumstance. Holiness despises sin, yet humility, regardless of sin, can have an expressive encounter with Holiness.

Humility, Grace, and Holiness these three, and yet the greatest of these is Holiness. Divine power decided to become a man and walk in flesh.

And then God chooses to do something that He had never done throughout all of His very existence; He chose to die. However, the grave does not have a death grip on Holiness. Holiness had to disrupt the true essence of its very divine power to go against the same law of divinity to dwell in a world of hatefulness and death, sickness and disease, and yet find humility and become intimate with unsanctified vessels just for the sake of making those vessels holy and perfect.

What happened to the Holiness preacher?

Why does Grace seem superior to Holiness?

Why is it that Holiness does not put Grace in check?

It appears that Grace is allowed to take advantage of Holiness, and humility has to step in between the two; that Holiness will not disenfranchise the entire kingdom.

Nevertheless, Grace wants to have its way by giving favor to undeserving souls. Such as the preacher preaching so much grace, and he does not have a lifestyle of holiness. *"I will Grace my way through the kingdom,"* says the preacher—humility steps in as a wife seducing her husband and takes a kiss with Holiness.

And says to **HIS HOLINESS**, allow it.

Now that's amazing... Amazing Grace!

And what's even more, this kiss will never end. I remember the day **When Humility Kissed Holiness** on my behalf.

EIGHT
"Satan's Seat"

I know where you live, where Satan has his throne. Yet you remain true to my name. You did not renounce your faith in me, not even the days of Antipas, my faithful witness, who was put to death in your city where Satan lives.—Revelation 2:13—NIV.

The Lord knows our address; uniquely, what He stated afterward is exceptionally thought-provoking. (Where Satan has his throne —Revelation 2:13). To allow us to see that we live in a satanic region dominated and controlled by the adversary himself. And execution and death is the prize for faithfulness, in Christ Jesus, what a paradox.

It is hard for a man to lose his soul. However, the fundamental perplexing dichotomy is how a preacher can lose his Faith. "I saw Satan fall like lightning from Heaven."—Luke 10:18—NIV.

"Therefore rejoice, you heavens and you who dwell in them in the presence of God. Woe to the earth and the sea because the devil has come down to you in great wrath, knowing that he has only a short time remaining!" Revelation 12:12—AMP.—paraphrased.

Notwithstanding now, the preacher has to develop the constant psychological profile of dealing with a defeated foe, Satan is defeated, and Jesus is triumphant. Satan is angry (because he knows he has a short time)—Revelation12:12.

A short time for what? Satan will be locked into the abyss for a thousand years, and his foolishness will cease. Then I saw an angel descending from heaven, he was holding the key of the abyss, the bottomless pit, and a great chain was in his hand. He gripped and overpowered the dragon, that old serpent of primeval times, who is the devil and Satan himself, and securely bound him for a thousand years. Then he hurled him into the abyss, the bottomless pit, and closed it and sealed it above him so that he could no longer lead astray, deceive and seduce the nation's until the thousand years were at an end. After that, he must be liberated for a short time. —Revelations 20:1; 3—AMP.

Here is a great mystery. Why would the Lord release the enemy even after a thousand years? Of course, if you are a pre-millennialist, you can answer this question. However, for those who are a-millennialist and post-millennial, this would be a catastrophic blunder on behalf of the Godhead to do such a thing. I believe this would fall in the category when Jesus said, "I have yet many things to say unto you, but ye cannot bear them now." —John 16:12. I believe it alludes to the great grace of God as to how He will give all of His creation an opportunity to be reconciled with Himself. Satan is the only one that will never have this opportunity.

Simply because there is no repentance found within him. So we believe, so we think. It leaves me to truly understand why Satan is so angry—Lucifer, his beautiful name the Daystar of Heaven the Cherub of God.

Heavenly Father was so unintimidated by creating such a being knowing that he would cause catastrophic chaos within the heavens. Yet, God still created him and gave him free will. The very thought itself is extremely perplexing, almost diabolical of Jehovah Himself; it seems that Heavenly Father was casting away evil out of His own being. "You are my witnesses, says the Lord, And My servant whom I have chosen, That you may know and believe Me, And understand that I Am He. Before Me there was no God formed, Nor shall there be after Me. I, even I, am the Lord, And besides Me there is no savior." —Isaiah 43:10-11—NKJV.

I form the light and create darkness, make peace national well-being, and create physical evil calamity. I am the Lord who does all these things.—Isaiah 45:7—AMP (paraphrased).

The Jewish Messiah preacher, Jesus, tells us, "Do not be afraid of those who kill the body but cannot kill the soul. Rather, be afraid of the One who can destroy both soul and body in hell". —Matthew 10:28—NIV.

We give too much power to Satan's Seat.

Nevertheless, we cannot ignore that the adversary has a seat. "The secret things belong to the Lord our God." —Deuteronomy 29:29. Only the Heavenly Father Himself knows why He allows this fallen cherub to even have a throne. The preponderance of the evidence is staggering and overwhelming that this once beautiful covering of God is now the Lord's greatest nemesis; oddly enough, we can still see the love of God.

We must truly ask ourselves the most challenging question, why won't God just stamp Satan out and destroy him into oblivion?

Why does this diabolical supreme demoniac have a place of noteworthiness that we should even discuss?

Why not focus on the faithfulness of Michael, the archangel, who is like God?

Who declared to the Prophet Daniel, "I Have Come For Your Words Daniel" —10:12.

Indeed, this great angel Michael deserves a throne seat. However, consider his great humility, consider his great strength. He loves and honors the Godhead fully.

Then war broke out in heaven. Michael and his angels fought against the dragon, and the dragon and his angels fought back. But he was not strong enough, and they lost their place in heaven. The great dragon was hurled down—that ancient serpent called the devil, or Satan, who leads the whole world astray. He was hurled down to the earth, and his angels with him. —Revelation 12:7-10—NIV.

But even the archangel Michael, when he was disputing with the devil (Satan), and arguing about the body of Moses, did not dare bring an abusive condemnation against him, but [simply] said, "The Lord rebuke you!"—Jude 9—AMP.

Is it possible that the Lord still loves His fallen son Lucifer? Indubitably sure, in religious circles, it is heretic considering such thoughts.

But wait, what happened to the preacher, who backslides and falls away from the faith?

Can he recover?

Will God restore him; of course, God can heal from the uttermost to the outer darkness. However, some are genuinely false prophets, lying, cheating, stealing, practicing all mannerisms of evil devices while standing in front of God's people with fermented evil and perversion coming out of their spirit and transforming sanctuaries into synagogues of Satan. Having the form of godliness while practicing witchcraft and deception.

"He will oppose and exalt himself over [against] everything that is called God or is worshiped, so that he sets himself up in God's temple, proclaiming himself to be God." 2 Thessalonians 2:4—NIV.

He will use all sorts of displays of power through signs and wonders that serve the lie, and all the ways that wickedness deceives those who are perishing. They perish because they refused to love the truth and so be saved. —2 Thessalonians 2:9b-10—NIV.

Here's an insight to those who worship the throne of Satan. They hate the truth, and a continuing lie lives in their spirit. Then there came out a spirit and 2 Chronicles 18:20-21—AMP.

So incredible is the permissive will of God.

To allow a man to proceed within his own devices. 'Let no one say when he is tempted, "I am being tempted from God," for God is incapable of being tempted by what is evil, and He Himself tempts no one. But every person is tempted when he is drawn away, enticed, and baited by his own evil desire, lust, and passion. "Then the evil desire, when it is conceived, gives birth to sin, and sin, when it is fully matured, brings forth death."' —James 1:13-15 AMP—paraphrased.

What is the infinity that men have with Death? What is the real controversy between God and Death? "But you must not eat of the tree of the knowledge of good and evil, for when you eat from it you will certainly die."—Genesis 2:17—NIV.

"You will not certainly die, the serpent said to the woman." —Genesis 3:4—NIV.

The Apostle Paul declares that death is God's last enemy. Thus, the last enemy to be destroyed is death. —1 Corinthians 15:26 —NIV.

Why is Death an enemy? Of course, the answer is simple, death is separation from God. However, what's the lustful lure of Satan's throne, besides the apparent profligacies, of power, money, and sexual lust. Even though these may be pleasurable sins, they are fleeting. —Hebrews 11:25-paraphrased

I have discovered the genuine desire of evil men; they too want to be worshipped.

Satan rose up against Israel and enticed David to take a census of Israel. —1Chronicles 21:1—NIV.

Again, the anger of the Lord burned against Israel, and He enticed David against them, saying, "go take a census of Israel and Judah." —2 Samuel 24:1—NIV.

"But Joab replied to the king, "May the Lord God multiply the troops a hundred times over, and may the eyes of my Lord the king see it. But why does my Lord the king want to do such a thing?" —2 Samuel 24:3—NIV.

Where are the Joab's in the life of the preacher? Simply to say, Pastor, don't do such a thing. Scholars have debated extensively as to what's going on in these two verses. In Chronicles and in Samuel, either the king is being used by Satan or Satan is a servant of the Lord.

If the king's heart is in the hand of the Lord Proverbs 21:1, why would the Lord allow such a thing?

Or how can the Lord be so enraged with Israel that He would use His king to do such a thing and then turn around and punish 70,000 men as an atonement?

God's ways are past finding out. However, the more I look into this, it appears that Satan is the Lord's fallen cherub, and even in his fallen state, God's goodness and love are even kind towards him.

We can only see but a glimpse into this supernatural eternal family. The Godhead: Gabriel, the word bearer; Michael, the war general; Lucifer, the fallen light-bearer, of praise and worship, who is now called the devil; the evil one. The Saints of God now hold that position: the light of the world and praise and worship.

Nevertheless, make no mistake, preacher, Satan's throne is good enough to be evil at its best. Unfortunately, some preachers choose Satan's seat. This eternal seat of evil has destroyed Nations and the greatest of ministers. Preacher, be careful where you SIT.

NINE
"When Preachers Pray"

In that night, God appeared to Solomon, and said to him, "Ask what I shall give you." —2 Chronicles 1:7—ESV.

Oh, Kind Heavenly Spirit. It is my prayer that you would appear unto me in the exact similitude and ask of me. I, too, would ask you for wisdom to walk about in your kingdom and nurture God's people with Godly knowledge, wisdom, understanding, and revelation. My heart would only seek to be pleasing and acceptable in your sight. I would have no desire for any self-seeking Glory of my own. My only desire would be to magnify the glory of the Lord. My inner desire would be to have acknowledgment and established manifestation from you, oh Kind Father, of that in which you sent me to the earth, to accomplish. Thus what can I give unto you, Kind Heavenly Spirit?

Now Jesus was praying in a certain place, and when he finished, one of his disciples said to him, "Lord, teach us to pray."—Luke 11:1—ESV.

Kind Loving Eternal Spirit, indeed Jesus has given us the gateway to heaven, with His prayer to His disciples, in which we in modernity do still follow. Holy Father, provide us with power when we release prayer utterance that formless energy will begin to manifest into that which we declare and decree. Formless manifestation, which is beneficial to the kingdom of God. The manifestation that's not of selfish nature.

Allow us to co-create in the architectural design of new heavens and a new earth in the spirit realm. Let doors be gateways into ancient dimensions of the Godhead. Let windows become the supernatural vision that we may see into the imagery of unfeigned Love that moves us into the position of our final destiny.

Let us love in sincerity and in truth. Joshua 24:15—ESV. And let us put away the false Gods in which we served before we came to accept and understand grace and the salvation of truth.

Help us, Kind Spirit, to put away the false God of racism hiding in the cloak of an evangelical believer. Give us the power to put away the false God of political delusions that contradicts the very written word of God.

Let politicians be politicians. Let preachers be preachers. Please forgive us, Kind Spirit, when we as preachers act like politicians.

Yes, Oh Lord, we have a responsibility to speak truth to the ordained powers. Nevertheless, we have strayed away as preachers when we allow ourselves to be captured by a faction of any political party that would cut us a check for the Preacher's influence.

However, it's an interesting paradox, money and the preacher. Prophet and preacher himself, Solomon declared that (money is the answer to everything)—Ecclesiastes 10:19—ESV.

Contextually, that only applies to things on earth. It also applies to those who would live outside of the will of God. And it does not matter your nationality or language. Money with wisdom answers everything, and I have a lot of questions. Money is not righteous; money is not wicked. The Bible says, "For the love of money is the root of all evil. —1 Timoty 6:10. But Rev. Frederick J. Eikerenkoetter II says, "the lack of money is the root of all evil."

Money is the answer in the earth realm aside from the Godhead.

However, "Yours, O LORD, is the greatness and the power and the glory and the victory and the majesty, for all that is in the heavens and in the earth is Yours. Yours is the kingdom, O LORD, and you are exalted as head above all." — 1 Chronicles 29:11—ESV.

Both riches and honor come to YOU, and YOU reign over All.

In Your hands are power and might. In Your hands, it is to make great, to give strength to all. Therefore, our God, we thank YOU and praise YOUR glorious name and those attributes that Thy Name denotes.

But who am I, and what are my people, that we should retain strength and be able to offer this so willingly? "For all things come from YOU, and out of YOUR own hand, we have given YOU." King David's Blessing.

"He saith, Yes. And when he was come into the house, Jesus prevented him, saying, What thinkest thou, Simon? of whom do the kings of the earth take custom or tribute? Of their own children or of strangers? Peter saith unto him, Of strangers. Jesus saith unto him, Then are the children free. Notwithstanding, lest we should offend them, go thou to the sea, and cast an hook, and take up the fish that first cometh up; and when thou hast opened his mouth, thou shalt find a piece of money: that take, and give unto them for me and thee."— Matthew 17:25-27.

Kind Loving Father, where is our sea of abundance, where is our deep catch, for we have worked all day, and our toll taxes are extremely heavy. Some days we have made nothing of our business and commerce. We have reduced our life to the farmer's cliche of "He may not come when you want Him, but He'll be there right on time."

Yet in Your Word, You have given Your apostle clear instructions as to where the hidden treasure shall be found. Father, tell us where to find it, tell us where to find our love, tell us where to find our wealth, tell us where to find happiness, tell us where to find our earthly prosperity, to stop the accusation of our accusers.

Father, You have declared that the children are free. It does not look good on us as children of God when we cannot pay our bills or are taxed in unjust ways. Yes, some of us have been unwise Stewart's, yet (your love is from everlasting to everlasting)—Psalms 103:17—ESV—paraphrased.

However, others have never attained a level of health, wealth, and prosperity, yet they call upon Your Name and in faithfulness more than those who are wicked, yet the wicked have material things for their lives.

Father, give us clarity and understanding as to why things are such and so, for we recognize that this world is not our home. Teach us and develop us into obtaining the answer to money.

Forge us into what You have declared for us that (we shall be the lender and not the borrower.) —Deuteronomy 28:12—ESV—paraphrased.

Reveal unto us the currency of Heaven. Disclose unto us the secret paths of eternal wealth in the manifestation of the material and spiritual display. Allow our eyes to see it, and let us pass it to our children in perpetuity. "Take us back to the garden where we knew no sin, take us back to the garden of way back when the days were peaceful and in the evening I would walk with you." —Robert Darby (songwriter).

Give us the memory of paradise Kind Heavenly Spirit. This physical world we once lived in will never be our Utopia. Allow us to see images of our celestial bodies as we Tabernacle on this terrestrial side of Your Glory. Give us droplets of the Tree of Life, increase our cognitive abilities to operate as sons of God, and we will occupy and have dominion of our territories until you return.

When the Lord returns, shall He find faith on earth?—Luke 18:8—ESV.

This oratorical statement, at best, within itself, is a rhetorical question posed by Jesus. For without faith, it is impossible to please God, for he that comes to God must believe that He is and that He is a rewarder of them that diligently seek Him. —Hebrews 11:6—ESV.

What is it that You, Oh Lord, would make an inquiry? People will have faith to fly on airplanes and never meet the pilot; they won't even know if they got drunk or high the night before their flight.

Doctors will perform surgeries, and the patient won't know if the surgeon did a line of cocaine hours before the operation. Multitudes of people will take the pandemic shot of the 2020 covid-19 vaccine. Millions of people will make purchases online, giving away their credit card numbers and account numbers. Oh yes, there's plenty of faith! However, this is a faith that is rooted in a system that will soon pass away. Shall the Lord find faith when He returns to the earth? —Luke 18:8 —NIV.

Kind Lord, why are you asking a question that you have the answer to? I see the reply Kind Heavenly Father, You are so amazing that You give rejoinder at the beginning of this allegory. Acknowledgment of faith is that "men ought always to pray and not faint."—Luke 18:1—ESV. Amen.

The Lord's abundant mercy has begotten us again unto a lively hope by the resurrection of Jesus Christ. —1 Peter 1:3 —ESV.

The controversy of doctrine in antiquity can now be put to rest. There is a resurrection.

Kind Heavenly Father, we are so grateful to be born of God. "To an inheritance incorruptible and undefiled and that fades not away." —1 Peter 3:4—ESV

You have preserved us, and You have reserved us by the word of Your power. And we are stored up like jars of good fruit for Your eternal glory. Allow us to taste good to men when we are seen in the marketplace. However, not for our own prestige and prominence, but that Your glory may be revealed in us as the saints of God. We are so thankful that you love us, it is amazing how you trust us, and you have placed us in Grace and called us to Ministry.

You covered transgressions about us despite what you knew about us. For Your love has established us. Look at what love has done for me. As we consider the number of times that we have fallen. And yet, You were right there. And we fell again. And yet, You were right there again. And we fell again. And You were STILL right there. Reviving us in the resurrection of Your Grace. Thank You, Kind Spirit.

I hear angels whispering in the trees. "We have walked to and fro through the earth, and, behold, all the earth sits still, and it is at rest.' —Zachariah 1:11—ESV-paraphrased.

Talking with angels in my lifetime, I pray I was all I need to be when that Heavenly stranger had a talk with me. We hear Your gentle Voice moving in the breeze. Some would think that You are so far away; however, You are very near. The way You have manifested Yourself in our very presence. When I was climbing Lifes mountains, I saw You, and I made it to the top and witnessed the glory of Your handiwork.

I have seen Christ in some unorthodox places. I saw Him sitting in the jail in a man that was so sorry for his crime, crying, stating that he would never do it again, and You released him.

I saw Him sitting in a man with HIV Aids, and He healed him. I have seen You turn harlots to holiness. I have seen you turn drug dealers into deacons. I have seen You turn pimps into pastors. I have seen You turn male whores into eunuchs, and they gave their lives to the kingdom of God. I have seen You take strippers off the pole and place them at the ecclesiastical desk of hope.

Can an Ethiopian change his skin or a leopard its spots? Neither can you do good who are accustomed to doing evil. —Jeremiah 13:23—NIV.

Kind Father, we cannot change who we are; it is only by the power of God that we even have the mind or the will within our heart to begin to change. But what will we change into? How shall we become new creatures according to Your word? Seeing that we are in a constant battle within the sinews of our human bodies.

Yes, Kind Lord, we have put away the weight of sin, but we pick the weight up again five years in the future. Only to feel the pain of guilt and shame, remembering the process repeatedly, we started when we asked You to remove our profligacy.

Kind Spirit, can our profligacy be used as a gift? Rahab was a harlot; Mary Magdalene was a woman of great seduction. Samson loved Philistine girls, and King Solomon loved strange women. Esther was the king's concubine for one year,

AKA side chick before they consummated a marriage.

Loving Father, how can our spots be so beautiful on the outside and so wretched on the inside? When will our consciousness match our beautiful spots?

The blessing of our decadence is a setup for God to lavish His love over circumstances we cannot change. The spots are there; the scars are permanent. And the spiritual makeover that we truly desire cannot take place on the outside. It is an inside transformation. It is an exchange of our internal fecklessness to become filled with faith in God's mercy concerning our messy outward blotches. God looked beyond the smudge and the smear and saw our need within, gave us the gift of Grace, and gave us salvation for sin. Father, we are so grateful for this internal exchange that extends the benefits of Your proliferous blessing to us regardless of our external blemishes.

It is with gratitude and meekness we accept the requite of our epidemiological disposition. "I cannot change the skin I'm in." I'll exchange my mind for God's pensiveness to live again.

What Happened to The Preacher

"Say it loud I'm Black, and I'm proud" —James Brown. God did not say that!

When preachers pray, how our minds may drift in the moment of a serious dissertation. Oh, how our minds drift while in the very presence of God. Heal us Kind Spirit from this spotted fever! We praise You for the refund of our redemption, and we are internally, externally, and eternally grateful to come into the full manifestation of your likeness. We Pray. Amen.

TEN
"HUGS HEAL"

We have been wrapped all of our existence. When God said, let us make man, Genesis 1:26 —ESV. The Lord embraced us in the Spirit realm. He has nurtured us as a loving, Kind Spirit; strangely, He Himself is the many breasted one El Shaddai.

We often view God as Father; however, we never considered Him as a mother. Yet, in our sermons, we confer upon Him as a Father to the fatherless and a mother to the Motherless. Friends to the homeless—a wheel within a wheel Ezekiel 1:16 ESV. And like a mother grabs her skirt and reaches down to wipe the snotty nose of her child. God has wiped sin off of man and hugged him in Grace. He has sealed and embraced His children with unconditional love. How is it then that we have become numb to this eternal embrace?

We have lost the sense of God's hand holding and reaching to retain us close to Him. Like spoiled children, we let go of His hand, and we run ahead of Him like a child takes off running in a shopping mall. Causing Him to chase after us as a loving parent. And when He catches us, He picks us up, and nozzles us to His bosom, and carry us under the pit of His arms; as a mother, we are propped up on the rose of her hip. And like spoiled brats, we throw tantrums to be released from the most secure position in our lives.

We break away from parental protection of a **Kind Heavenly Spirit**, saying to Him I can do it all by myself. Surprisingly, He allows us to run unconfined while we make declarations of being unapologetically liberated.

As God's preachers, the result for us is that we too can find ourselves in a faraway place simply because we despised a Father's embrace. (Even if you had countless guardians in Christ, you do not have many fathers, for, in Christ Jesus, I became your father through the gospel. Therefore, I urge you to imitate me.—1 Corinthians 4:15-16 ESV. —paraphrased.

What Happened to The Preacher

We have given witness to our earthly spiritual fathers in the gospel. Many of our church fathers taught us an oral gospel handed down because of the lack of education. When the opportunity to be educated was awarded, there was a lack of respect and disdain for the seminarian prognosticator.

The controversy of the educated preacher is that his education makes him too liberal and militant or too conservative and racist. Needless to say, no one wishes to embrace this doctrine on either scale. The Apostle Paul was highly educated yet extremely belligerent and prejudiced before his conversion. The Apostle Peter had no education, save the University of Christ Jesus Himself, yet still faced racism after his conversion. "These men have been with Jesus" —Acts 4:13—ESV.

Consequently, this is where factions and divisions have taken a stronghold. Subsequently, new prophetic movements are departing the mainstream denominations. Publicly we have watched our spiritual mentors ascend to greatness and fall to disgrace. And no one wishes to accept them on the bottom after the fall. Nevertheless, the Oil of God is still running in that preacher. Should we make them sit on the sidelines; or expelled them from the ministry?

How do we help the preacher recover after his divorce that was so public?

How do we help him get rid of the drug scandal that landed him in prison?

How do we help them recover from sex addiction?

Is there recuperation of one's esteemed recognition? Who will HUG these men and women of God after such ignominy?

Elegance coupled with poise, enfolded with finesse and charm traced with politeness and good manners, honor crowned with distinction, can't measure to the eternal grasp of Grace. Is Grace the healing HUG? If so, how is it exercised among believers and non-believers? Understanding that this concept had to be taught to our human consciousness. Extending Grace is the appropriate responsibility for the devoted disciple. However, it will make one look foolish to a non-believer. It is baffling anxiety even to some believers; nevertheless, the Holy One desires to HUG us and hold us and never let us go.

"How shall we escape if we ignore so great a salvation? This salvation, which was first announced by the LORD, was confirmed to us by those who heard him. God also testified to it by signs, wonders and various miracles, and by gifts of the Holy Spirit distributed according to his will."—Hebrews 2:3-4—ESV.

Children can drift away from what their parents have taught them. Men and women of God can drift away from the essential rudiments and the fundamental elements of the Gospel. Which is "Jesus saves from the utmost." —Hebrews 7:25—ESV.

Why would we gravitate away from holiness that would heal us into happiness, allowing a fallen believer to sense the joy of redemption? When children are hurt, they typically sob and wail to their parents with open arms with an expectation to be picked up, coddled, and encouraged. Delightfully it is the desire of Jehovah to spoil his sons and daughters with love and kisses and hugs. "The Lord is good to all, and all His Mercy is over all that he has made." —Psalms 145:9—ESV.

Regardless of education or high pedigree with a degree, or no formal matriculation, only the Lord can make a preacher.

The Lord will encapsulate you, and because He is our Loving Father, He is the only disciplinarian to restoration. After which it will be the homiletics of your life that will write your sermons integrated with the truth of hermeneutics forged from your pain, embarrassment, and reclamation that will cause you to embrace the text in its true interpretation, as it relates to the dispensation wherein you now live. Allowing you to speak to your generation with brazenness and clarity, not seeking the acquiescence and accolades of men. Even so, focused on understanding directives endorsed by the Holy Spirit. Nothing will be squandered; every setback will be reestablished with a firm conviction that God will still use you despite your problems.

Life is not a sprint; life is a relay of toleration while walking in the shoes of sufferance, thoughtfully bearing the burdens of one another while simultaneously fortifying the citadel of your own heart. All things in the watercourse of existence will dissolve into their final rivers. "And it came to pass" bible text quotes will begin to be the continual subject matter, as "work out your own soul salvation with fear and trembling."—Philippians 2:12—ESV.

Consider the trust of God that He would certify us as preachers to do a self-examination of psychology to our very own soul. Servant (Preacher) be assiduous in regards to your locution. Heaven is listening, and your words will embrace you to heal or castigate you into obscurity.

Prescient opinions will escalate and de-escalate. The school of consciousness as to how God is proceeding will come under great speculation. Men will begin to hold the philosophy of human secularism as their devotion to God. Consider prayerful admonishment preacher and be encouraged to turn away from worldly allegiances, conceptualized with sorcery roots. These allegiances will promote false agendas. Such as:

"We don't have to worship God."

"There is more than one way to God."

"Jesus is not the only way."

"It's okay if I dress this way."

"Excuse me, but I'm unapologetically me." And "I'm an alternate, and I'm saved."

Prophetic Ministries need biblical apologetics for trepidation that they will be hugging and seated in the lap of the evil one. "Now, the spirit expressively says that in latter times some will depart from the Faith by devoting themselves to deceitful spirits and teachings of demons through the insincerity of liars and those whose consciences are seared." —1 Timothy 4:1-2—ESV.

Beloved, have you ever seen someone you love hugged up with the wrong person? God is a jealous GOD. —Exodus 34:14—ESV.

He wants you back preaching about Him.

I desire then that men should pray, lifting holy hands without anger or quarreling in every place. —1 Timothy 2:8—ESV. Picture when you lift your hands, you say to God and men that there is nothing in my hands that would harm you. After raising hands, men in antiquity would embrace shoulder to shoulder to continue the peace vouchsafe. Indicating that there are no weapons between them to destroy one another. When the gospel is preached, it must demonstrate with open arms that the Christ of God and His power can embrace any circumstance in our lives and that Christ is a safe haven of amelioration and reimposition.

Uniquely the Lord spoke to King Solomon, a preacher, in the long ago to everything there is a season and a time and a purpose under the heaven. — Ecclesiastes 3:1—ESV.

"Time to embrace a time to refrain from embracing." —Ecclesiastes 3:5—ESV.

Why embrace; why not embrace?

If you listen, you will be able to hear the hunger pains of millions on the planet. A meal, a hug, and I love you will start a dialogue of fellowship. If you listen, you will feel the cold and the heat of thousands of homeless sleeping in the streets and under bridges. Food, clothes, shelter, and a warm embrace, will change the countenance of their day. If you listen carefully, a random stranger will tell you how a friend or a loved one hurt them, and they are struggling with the pain of betrayal and disappointment.

If you listen, you will hear the cry of men who know not God, and yet their secret desire is to discover Him. If you listen, you will hear the cry of a single mother who can't pay her bills, and her body is now a consideration for payment in full. If you listen closely, you will hear the cries of the elderly who are lonely with no one to talk to, wondering if God has forgotten all about them. If you listen close, you will hear the cry of a preacher in need of prayer.

Beloved, can I give you a Hug?

Beloved preacher, the world is going to need you to be a pharos of light. A sounding board to holiness, a firebrand turning the righteous away from wickedness. Good preachers are not cheap and cheap preachers are not good. He that has an ear. Selah.

The patterns of how you live your life will be significantly scrutinized in the public courts of television, radio, and social media platforms. Even your beloved constituent of saints will whisper things about you. Some of the rumors will be true, and it is you who will try to conceal your discreditability.

On the other hand, there will be lies, conspiracies, and concocted schemes set for your demise. Nevertheless, the Lord has prepared your exculpation. And when you get to your secret place, take the hug that will heal your Ministry.

Take the hug that will heal your marriage.

Take the hug that will heal your finances.

Take the hug that will heal your mental illness.

Take the hug that will make you whole again.

Preach the word, be ready in season and out of season, reprove, rebuke, and exhort with complete patience and teaching.

"People will not endure sound teaching for the time will come, but having itching ears will allow teachers to suit their own passions and turn away from listening to the truth and wander off into fables and myths. —II Timothy 4:2-4—ESV. —paraphrased.

Why preacher, what happened? What Happened to The Preacher? God's servant to tell it like it is, don't be afraid of the repercussions for your candor. Popularity is not your friend; the truth is your friend; live for your king, clinch a grappling hook to your mantle in Christ. Unequivocally with no fear, warn the people, encourage the saints, JESUS is Coming.

Preach preacher!!!!

ABOUT THE AUTHOR

George A. Gee is a native of Indianapolis, Indiana. He studied at Heritage Christian University, Florence, Alabama, for three and a half years. South Florida Theological Seminary, MDiv program a year and a half. And last but not least, Southwest Bible Tech Institute of Huntsville, Alabama.

George received his call and was anointed at a young age, privileged to have experience in ministry service. With 32 years of ministry, George has served the Body of Christ in Alabama, Florida, and Indiana, as senior pastor and co-pastor and currently serves Christanointed Ministries in Houston, Texas. He has worked extensively across multi denominations, advancing ecumenism of unity following the direction of the Holy Spirit.

George is a National Recording Artist, well heard with 10 million units sold and honored to be a United States Marine Corps Military Veteran.

About the Author

From the ecclesiastical desk with didactic teaching to the darkest alley riddled with the smell of urine and feces, this preacher (George Gee) knows that God can save mankind from every conundrum.

www.ingramcontent.com/pod-product-compliance
Lightning Source LLC
Chambersburg PA
CBHW071136090426
42736CB00012B/2132